THE NATURAL VS. HUMAN CAUSES OF AIR POLLUTION

ENVIRONMENT TEXTBOOKS

Children's Environment Books

BABY PROFESSOR
EDUCATION KIDS

Speedy Publishing LLC
40 E. Main St. #1156
Newark, DE 19711
www.speedypublishing.com

In this book, we're going to talk about the natural versus the human causes of air pollution. So, let's get right to it!

Morning smoke from factories with rising sun.

WHAT IS AIR POLLUTION?

There's nothing more wonderful to breathe than fresh, clean air. However, it's hard to find locations where the air is completely pure anymore. In many cities and even in the country, you can see the pollution in the air.

The air we breathe is part of Earth's atmosphere. The atmosphere keeps our planet protected from the searing heat of the Sun and its solar wind and radiation. Without clean air, we can't survive. Air pollution is caused when toxic gases, fine dust particles, smoke, fumes, or unpleasant smells get into the atmosphere. These pollutants are harmful to people as well as to animals and plants.

View of a very foggy Hong Kong.

There are many different types of pollutants. *Here are some of the common types:*

- **NITROGEN OXIDES,** from burning fuel

- **CARBON MONOXIDE,** from car exhaust

- **HYDROCARBONS,** from burning oil

- **SULFUR DIOXIDES,** from burning coal

- **FINE PARTICLES OF SAND OR DUST,** from leaf-blowing or other causes

- **ORGANIC COMPOUNDS,** from household cleansers and disinfectants

Pollution.

TWO TYPES OF POLLUTANTS

There are two types of pollutants—primary and secondary. Primary pollutants are the types that are emitted directly into the air and immediately cause pollution. An example of a primary pollutant is carbon monoxide. It comes directly out of car exhausts as the cars burn gasoline fuel. Sulfur dioxide is another type of primary pollutant. It goes into the air as soon as coal is burned.

Cars at Rush Hour Driving Through Thick Smog.

When chemicals get into the air, they sometimes mix with other chemicals and cause reactions. The end result of these reactions are often chemicals that are even more dangerous than the original chemicals. An example of a secondary pollutant is photochemical smog. It's a type of air pollution that's caused when radiation from the Sun reacts with pollutants in the atmosphere such as nitrogen oxides.

Los Angeles Smog.

Air pollution by power plant.

WHY IS AIR POLLUTION AN IMPORTANT ENVIRONMENTAL ISSUE?

Air pollution is dangerous to your health. It's also dangerous to the overall environment and it hurts the economy too.

AIR POLLUTION IS DANGEROUS TO YOUR HEALTH

Breathing of polluted air causes cancer as well as lung injuries. Toxic chemicals in the atmosphere also cause damage to our brains and our nervous systems. Pregnant women who breathe toxic air are putting their unborn children at risk for birth defects.

The air is so polluted in some areas that people can't go outside without suffering from their eyes and noses running. The air quality is sometimes so poor that it triggers problems with people who have trouble breathing. People with asthma are particularly susceptible. Air is so polluted in some areas that people have died from breathing it.

Girl wearing mouth mask with filter against air pollution, Beijing.

Over 40% of the people in the United States are currently living in areas that have polluted air on a regular basis. Childhood asthma is on the rise with over 30% of the cases directly caused by toxic exposure in the environment.

Portrait of little boy wearing modern pollution mask.

AIR POLLUTION IS DANGEROUS TO THE ENVIRONMENT

When chemicals get into the atmosphere, they can cause acid rain. Acid rain is primarily caused by the burning of fossil fuels. When these waste gases, with their high concentration of sulfur as well as nitrogen oxides, combine with the water in the atmosphere, the rain that is formed is toxic. Acid rain pollutes the waterways making them unsafe for humans and animals.

Dead trees in forest.

AIR POLLUTION CAUSES PROBLEMS FOR THE ECONOMY

In order to have a healthy economy, people need to be healthy, because the economy is driven by the work performed by people. Air pollution makes people sick and it also reduces the healthy yields of crops and forests. Billions of dollars are lost annually because of air pollution.

Young woman wearing a mask in the smoggy city.

NATURAL CAUSES OF AIR POLLUTION

Some natural events can pollute the quality of our air. For example, powerful volcanic eruptions can spew ash and toxic chemicals into the air. Forest fires and the erosion of soil and rock by wind can also cause air pollution. Sometimes excessive amounts of pollen from plants can cause air pollution too.

Scenic air shot of Calbuco Volcano erupting.

Organic compounds evaporate into the air naturally and there's also a certain amount of radioactivity from the Sun that our atmosphere can't totally block out. However, most of the natural events eventually balance out. When manmade chemicals are absorbed into the atmosphere in large numbers, the air becomes toxic.

Activity at Mount Bromo in the early morning.

Winter landscape during sunset with steaming factory.

MANMADE CAUSES OF AIR POLLUTION

There are three main causes of manmade pollutants.

WASTES FROM MANUFACTURING

If you've ever seen the big smoke stacks from a factory, then you've witnessed the pollutants that they put into the air. Incinerators that burn wastes, factories and plants that manufacture and then release their waste chemicals into the air, and power plants all emit chemicals.

They also release carbon monoxide into the air. It's rare to live in an area where you don't see some evidence of this type of pollution. Refineries that create products from petroleum release dangerous hydrocarbons into the atmosphere as well.

Dirty Smoke Stacks Belch Carbon and Pollution into the Atmosphere.

BURNING OF FOSSIL FUELS

As our world population grows, so does our need for more cars, buses, and trucks. The emissions from our transportation vehicles are a major cause of both types of pollutants, primary and secondary. Trains, ships, and airplanes all burn types of fossil fuels as well. Vehicles are a major source of air pollution. It's a difficult type of pollution to control, because transportation is so important to our cities. We need vehicles to go from place to place as well as for goods and services.

Air pollution from vehicle exhaust pipe on road.

If you've ever smelled the fumes created from a car or a bus, you'll know right away that those fumes are toxic by the smell they give off. Hydrocarbons and nitrogen oxide are two of the chemicals created by car exhaust. So are hydrocarbons and a complex mix of dust, soot, smoke, liquid, and pollen, which is called particulate matter. Every vehicle that burns fossil fuel is putting pollutants into the air. In addition, once these pollutants get into the air, they combine with gases in the environment to create more types of toxic gases.

Traffic.

CHEMICALS USED ON FARMS AND IN HOUSEHOLDS

Crop dusting is used on farms to kill insects, but depending on the type of insecticide being used, it can be very polluting to the environment. Even over-the-counter cleaning supplies or supplies used for painting can be dangerous to people and cause pollution.

Crop duster plane banking over a field while spraying.

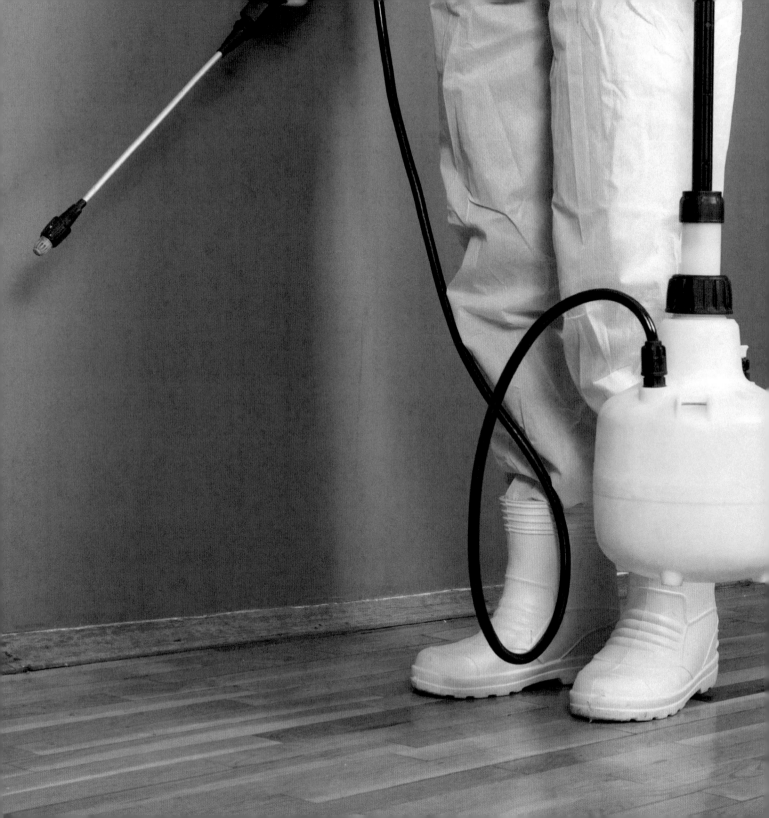

Sometimes we use these indoors at our homes and offices without the proper ventilation, which can cause us to become ill if we breathe them in. There are many nontoxic types of cleaners at the grocery store, so it makes sense to buy something that won't make you or your pets sick inside your home.

Pest Control Professional.

WHAT ENVIRONMENTAL PROBLEMS ARE CAUSED BY AIR POLLUTION?

Air pollution causes environmental problems that are very difficult to solve. Once the pollutants are in the air, they are hard to get rid of. Preventing the air from getting polluted in the first place is a better strategy.

There are *four major effects caused by air pollution.*

- Acidification

- Eutrophication

- Ozone at the Ground Level

- Various Forms of Particulate Matter

Dead Trees.

ACIDIFICATION

Acid rain is formed when chemicals like sulfuric acid from factory waste mix with water droplets in the atmosphere. This harmful type of rain kills trees and plants and if it falls in large quantities into bodies of water it can kill the animals and plants that live there.

Stagnant water with dead branches of trees emerging.

EUTROPHICATION

When nitrogen compounds get into the atmosphere and mix with rain, the resulting pollutants have a bad effect on the soil and water. This mixture sometimes results in an increase in the growth of algae in waterways. When there is too much algae, it can use up the oxygen in the water and deplete it, so other organisms can't survive.

Murky algae water.

OZONE AT THE GROUND LEVEL

Ozone is important at upper levels of the atmosphere because it blocks out harmful radiation from the Sun. However, at ground level, ozone can be dangerous because it's toxic for humans to breathe. Ozone, also called O_3 is created when pollutants mix with sunlight in the atmosphere.

Earth globe against planet map.

VARIOUS FORMS OF PARTICULATE MATTER

Particulate matter comes in lots of different shapes and sizes. The particles can range from 2.5 micrometers to 10 micrometers. About 40 of the 2.5-micrometer-size particles would fit along the width of a human hair. This type of pollution is very dangerous. It causes many types of respiratory conditions and can also cause headaches and nausea even when the exposure is only short term.

Young woman with face mask in the street.

People who have allergies, asthma, or emphysema are at risk when there is particulate matter in the air. Long-term effects are even more dangerous. Breathing in air pollution on a continuous basis can cause cancer and damage to the nervous system. Indoor pollution can be very dangerous too. Many people die each year from exposure to smoke on a continuous basis indoors. Smoking is very dangerous for the person who smokes and if someone lives with a smoker and is breathing in second-hand smoke all the time, he or she can get very ill as well.

Cigarette End.

Environmentalists and governments are doing their part to make sure that air pollution is prevented. We take in air at the rate of 20,000 liters every day, so it's critical that our air remains clean for us and for future generations.

Awesome! Now you know more about air pollution and its causes. You can find more Environment books from Baby Professor by searching the website of your favorite book retailer.

Visit

BABY PROFESSOR
EDUCATION KIDS

www.BabyProfessorBooks.com

to download Free Baby Professor eBooks and view
our catalog of new and exciting Children's Books

Made in the USA
Monee, IL
24 June 2021